IN THE ECHOEY TUNNEL

Christopher Reid was born in 1949. His first two collections
of poems, *Arcadia* (1979) and *Pea Soup* (1982), were
published by Oxford University Press, and his third,
Katerina Brac (1985), by Faber and Faber. He received an
Eric Gregory Award in 1978 and, on the publication of his
first book, a Somerset Maugham Award and a
Hawthornden Prize. His translation of Ödön von Horváth's
Figaro Gets Divorced, done in collaboration with János
Bruck, was performed in London in 1989. In 1991 he was
appointed Poetry Editor at Faber and Faber. He lives in
London and is married to the actress and patchwork-quilt
maker, Lucinda Gane.

by the same author

ARCADIA (Oxford University Press)
PEA SOUP (Oxford University Press)
KATERINA BRAC (Faber and Faber)

CHRISTOPHER REID
In the Echoey Tunnel

faber and faber
LONDON · BOSTON

First published in 1991
by Faber and Faber Limited
3 Queen Square London WC1N 3AU

Phototypeset by Wilmaset, Birkenhead, Wirral
Printed in England by Clays Ltd, St Ives plc

A CIP record for this book is available from the
British Library.

ISBN 0 571 16254 1
ISBN 0 571 16252 5 (hbk)

Contents

To the memory of my father,
and for my mother.

ACKNOWLEDGEMENTS

The author is glad to acknowledge the kindness of the editors of the following publications, where some of these poems, or versions of them, first appeared: *Grand Street, London Review of Books, Paris Review, Pequod, Poetry Book Society Anthology 1988/9, Soho Square 2, Times Literary Supplement* and *Verse*. A section of 'Memres of Alfred Stoker' was included in the *Faber Book of Vernacular Verse* edited by Tom Paulin. 'Contretemps' was broadcast on BBC Radio 3 in an edition of *Poetry Now* presented by John Fuller.

In the Echoey Tunnel

The little girl squealing
in the echoey tunnel,

scampering and squealing
just for the thrill of it,

spanking the pathway
with her own stampede of footfalls

and squealing, squealing
to make the brickwork tingle –

how fiercely she exults
in her brand-new discovery,

the gift of the tunnel
and its echoey gloom!

And then what a cheat,
to be dragged back to daylight!

A View of the Playground

Out on the playground someone was producing bubbles:
      not the small ones you get
      by breathing through a spoon-sized hole,
but enormous creatures, perhaps even a yard across.

It was too far to make out what the apparatus was,
      but where their filmy skins caught the light
      you could see them writhe and roll
off and up into the air with mighty shudders and wobbles.

People came to watch them. Their lives were so wretchedly
  brief,
      their passing so abrupt,
      it was hard not to admit
to some dark significance in their dumb carnival.

And I suspect all our hearts floated with them, until,
      growing too sausage-shaped,
      or at the mercy of a trembling fit,
they would burst with the peremptoriness of a sneeze or a
  cough.

I could have stood at the window all afternoon,
      utterly beguiled
      by this most otherworldly of peepshows,
but then a teenaged boy, rather fat and muscular, raced up.

He began throwing himself about in his wild efforts to pop
      as many fragile monsters as he could.
      I hated him at once, and I suppose
others did too, but nobody, I noticed, attempted to intervene.

Thy Doom

Some afternoons all London goes mad —
    and I don't mean just the odd bearded weirdo
        who stands on an island denouncing buses,
    or skew-whiff old biddy with institution hair-do
        looking like a lost child so far from her nurses;
but the whole city, all London, goes mad.

You feel it could well be the end of everything.
    The sky grieves under its load of darkness
        and the rules of perspective seem about to be broken,
    leaving each person with his/her separate sickness —
        a trancelike estrangement from which no one will
            waken
if this is, as you suspect, the end of everything.

Amphibiology

Like old men frolicking in sacks
seals slither on the sea-thrashed rocks.

Why does their melancholy sport
exert such a strong pull on my heart?

I could stand here for hours on end
watching them fail to make dry land.

From time to time one gains brief purchase,
adopting the pose of a Grand Duchess.

In seconds, though, a fist of surf
rises to swipe the pretender off.

Repetitive slapstick, it has the charm
of earliest documentary film.

Stuffed statesmen and wind-up warriors
turn to salute us across the years . . .

Only, in this case, something far
more ancient seems to hang in the air.

It could be the question, whether to plump
for a great evolutionary jump

or stay put in the icy brine.
May the good Lord send them a hopeful sign!

Contretemps

One lunchtime two men got in a fight.
The first tried to land a punch, but he missed.
Next moment, a barstool tipped and crashed,
the whole pub dropped to a dead hush and a tight

little space like a night-club dance floor grew
around the two bruisers in their ungainly clinch.
It was not like the movies: there was no second punch
and no attempt at fancy throwing. All they could do

was to totter on the spot, mutually clamped, grunting
and sputtering oaths, until one tripped and down
they both fell, still grappling. Each wore a frown
as stubborn as the other's. It recalled something

I'd seen long ago in a wild-life programme about
one of those grim, antiquatedly-armoured species
for whom the sexual act, through a whim of nature's,
has been made almost impossible to carry out.

Episode

Toddling from the 'Harvest Bar'
into the brash glare of two-thirty,
he found this message on his car:
        I AM DIRTY.

'Too true!' he thought, and with his fist
half-rubbed it out; then, tyres burning,
made for the motorway, but missed
        a vital turning.

The bodgy farmsteads and twee spires
of unknown England – bright clouds high
over interchangeable shires –
        sped him by.

And what did the night hold? Clearly, alas,
he saw the inevitable scene:
dim hotel lamp, a sinking glass
        and a magazine.

Hotels

In the first hotel
I opened my wardrobe
to an ambush from childhood:
a sweet, tugging fragrance
I couldn't name.
Shuttered windows
gave on to a blind drop
and the portamenti
of amorous cats.

*

In the second hotel
I noted that the wallpaper,
although of a strictly
geometrical pattern,
was upside-down.
A hornet arrived
the following morning,
loose-jointed, like a gunslinger.
Then it flew away.

*

In the third hotel
none of the corridors
ran into each other
quite where expected.
My Gideon Bible
was marked at *Lamentations*
by an envelope addressed
to Mrs Minnie Fireberg,
Utica, NY.

*

In the fourth hotel
I fell asleep
about nine o'clock.
Woke five hours later.
A woman in the street
was practising her giggling.
A bottle smashed.
Dawn crawled slowly
with its traffic chorus.

*

In the fifth hotel
the complimentary stationery
carried the most
vainglorious letterhead
I have ever seen.
Why didn't I steal some?
The plumbing shuddered
in every limb
at the twist of a single tap.

*

In the sixth hotel
the phone was pink
and its weight felt wrong
as I lifted the receiver.
It was no one I knew.
Advice and prohibitions
in several languages
were posted by the lightswitch
in a passepartout frame.

Caretaking
for Jane and Bernard McCabe

The seven-storey trees
on the jogger-thronged hill
beyond your back garden
register the breeze
with a convulsive thrill
of all their bright foliage,
a lightening of their burden
that I in turn acknowledge,
seated at your desk,
with the opulent awakening
of my own nerve-tree —
just in time to see
some strange woman beckoning,
her dog's doggy burlesque.

*

Following Maisie's
half-remembered map
of companionable smells,
obliged to stop
for the frequent delectation
of savoury breezes,
at last we reach the hill's
celebrated elevation
and there for a while we stand
with the usual kites flying,
joggers jogging,
lovers snogging,
and London itself lying
in the palm of the land.

*

Book shut, light out —
then in the gap
before real sleep
you feel the hill
looming closer,
then closer still,
a dreamlike imposture
that brings the trees'
lulling furor
right up to your ear,
and the monologue
of a distant dog
who more or less agrees
with what you have always thought.

One Star in the Michelin

The house at Giverny has been turned into a museum,
supported, you learn at the gate, by American funds.
A few francs get you into both house and grounds.
The main attraction is the celebrated garden,
Monet's home-made paradise, planted and painted by him
       through the optical haze
       of his long last days,
and now restored to trim after years of abandon.

We went in early October, when river mist –
or a fine drizzle – damped everything. Cosmos,
path-smothering nasturtium, stiff autumn crocus
and clumps of busy Lizzie were in full bloom.
The effect was Japanese-cum-Impressionist:
       a controlled disorder
       at every border,
the whole canvas organised with immaculate aplomb.

The water-garden is a separate area
which you reach through a tunnel under the main road,
stepping into a disconcertingly familiar world.
On our visit, although the lily-pads
had lost their crowns and the stout grey wisteria,
       lashed to its trellis,
       was now flowerless,
remembered visions shimmered about our heads.

Following the path around a bush, we halted
as abruptly as if we had seen a ghost.
A lawn-sprinkler twirled its spray into the mist

as if to replenish it, just where the old fellow
himself no doubt stood in his tweeds and contemplated
      the rainbow bridge,
      the tousled sedge,
the oriental fish and the weeping willow.

Tyger

       Early one frost-spiked morning
I was walking north from Golden Square
       in Soho, when – quite without warning –
I saw a troop of men appear
       around a corner, dragging what seemed
to be a full-grown tiger in a cage.
       Was it something I had dreamed?
It looked authentic enough: a huge
       potential man-eater that displayed
its amber teeth in a masklike snarl,
       while at the other end its tail swayed
time-bidingly . . .
                  Well,
       I stood back and let them pass –
the beast on its rope-drawn carriage
       and the men heaving with less fuss
than if it had been so much inert luggage.
       Where had they come from? Where were they bound?
The tarty boutiques and design studios
       cluttering that part of town
were all shut up; ditto, the hideous,
       tear-stained, granite-clad, sixties block
whose steps are graced, you may remember,
       by a sign saying, 'WILLIAM BLAKE
WAS BORN ON 28 NOVEMBER
       1757
IN A HOUSE WHICH STOOD ON THIS SITE'.

       So was it reality or vision?
Or just a trick of the morning light?

Two Teachers

Jolly Miss Chard
    taught us 'Hangman' –
        her utterly compelling
game of spelling,
    where a simple gallows
        grew on the blackboard

strut by strut
    as we made our mistakes,
        until every stick limb
of the innocent victim
    dangled before us
        and the final foot

showed he was dead.
    Such hilarious dismay
        greeted the coup de grâce
that the excited class
    could generally persuade
        nice Miss Chard

to begin again.
    Solemn Mr Talbot
        was in charge of sixth-formers –
all those enormous
    twelve-year-olds –
        but he once stood in

for poor Miss Chard
    when she was off sick.
        He showed us a toy
that he had made as a boy:
    a little square box
        of painted wood

with a glass panel
    set in the top,
        like one of those gizmos
that tend to appear at Christmas,
    in which a silver ball
        wobbles along a runnel

before the player
    loses control
        and it drops to its doom.
Young Talbot's theme
    had been *Pilgrim's Progress*.
        With exquisite care

he had fashioned the route
    from the City of Destruction
        to the Celestial City,
with numerous witty
    devices to stand
        for the Wicket Gate,

the Slough of Despond,
    Vanity Fair
        and the whole rigmarole.
The tiddly ball
    completed the journey
        in his wrinkled hand.

French Cricket

The too speedily
flickering pulse
of old celluloid
between spools . . .

Odour of singed
house-dust rising
with its ambiguous greeting
from the machine . . .

All pictures
and knick-knacks removed,
that patch of wallpaper
again receives

the impermanent
but transfixing imprint
of a time that was:
the pageant and fuss

of by-gone, bourgeois
heyday afternoons
on picnic verges
and tennis lawns –

all that sunlight
unreliably translated
to the sputter and glare
operative here,

that can incandesce
without notice
and blot out an entire scene.
As when

some young girl
in high-waisted frock
and ankle socks,
lobbing a ball,

would remain swaying
for a few seconds
on one leg,
piquantly displaying

her emphatic *ensellure*.

Consulting the Oracle

An old, slow and sometimes forgetful lift
takes you up to her flat on the eighth floor.
You carry in your hand some trivial gift,
ready to thrust at her inside the door.

It is accepted and then promptly hidden
in the kitchen, where you have never been.
You'd like to peep, just once, but this is forbidden
by the laws of a now fixed routine.

She comes out with the tea things on a tray
and you go with her down the unlit hall
to the front room with its museumlike display
of gilt-framed studio photographs on each wall.

Conversation gets off to a limp start.
The unreliable buses. Yesterday's snow.
What the new doctor says about her heart.
An aeroplane passes disconcertingly low.

You wonder why you've bothered, until by chance
your eye lights on a china hummingbird
and instantly she understands that glance
as an appeal. The oracle is stirred.

*It was one of a pair. Its precious twin
was stolen by the soldiers. All the time
her uncle stood there clutching this one in
his big fist – so!* She does a little mime.

With such authenticity, she too laughs.
You know that prim frown, that tilt of the head,
from numerous dressy family photographs,
most of whose subjects are, of course, long dead.

They can be traced from one frame to another:
the plump, horse-loving cousin who was raped . . .
the argumentative great-aunt . . . the lost brother . . .
the uncle in whose Daimler she escaped . . .

But that's enough. There will be more next time.
You bite a biscuit and sip from your cup.
Chit-chat makes do until the wheezy chime
of five o'clock, whereupon you stand up.

And your departure follows a strict pattern,
with steps down the hall, coat on, and always three
kisses bringing you to the lift's black button,
which you jab more than once, jogging its memory.

Pips

(after Katerina Brac)

Knowledge

it's the cleverest trick
Eve taught Adam

you bite the pip
and taste the whole tree

Us

2

the way you write it
almost like a question mark

Company

it never lasts
but for a while you have
the cat's deep
satisfied engine
turning over

Uplift

the village bus
surmounts
the humpback bridge

Forebodings

the cows all pointing one way
weathercockwise

intimations of thunder
in my little toe

Small Hours

the studious anglepoise
must have that blank sheet
off by heart

Romanesque

The Lion of Adultery
comes pouncing down.

His eyes bulge menacingly;
his mane is a blaze

of little slick flame-tufts.
Under his impending paw

a woman stands
whispering, animatedly,

words of love
into an office telephone.

*

You see a lawn
in Arcadia
or Suburbia.

Dapper, bearded,
two Centaurs lift
nimble forelegs to drum
the earth's taut tum.

With blithe smiles,
they represent
the innocence of the world
on a Bank Holiday Monday.

*

By the moon and padlock
it must be night
and a dangerous part of town.

One of the Unnamed Martyrs
hurries home
while, out of sight,

three club-clutching bugaboos
lie doggo.

They are King Yobbo
and his frenzied entourage.

*

A sort of Dandy Dinmont,
head cocked,
spouts like an orator.

This is the Miracle
(locally attested)
of the Dog that Spoke.

Out of the blue
he gave utterance
to all manner of mysteries.

The stars, medicine
and Holy Writ
were among the subjects he covered.

And what he said
his mistress jotted down
on the backs of old, torn envelopes.

*

The story here
remains obscure,
but the man and woman
who stand in the mouth
of the great, gaping fish –
horned and dragonish –
and peer over its teeth
as from a tiny back garden,
seem less afraid
than might have been expected.

*

Saint Quotidianus,
a taxi-driver in life,
appears with his emblem –
a steering-wheel.

He is flanked by the Angels
who showed him the true path:
one carries a trumpet,
the other a scrip.

Balloonland

In Balloonland
everyone
is given a balloon
the day they are born.

Freshly blown-up
and with the knot tightly done,
a big balloon
is put into their hand.

A few words are spoken
by way of ceremony:
'This is your balloon,
the balloon of your destiny!
You are its guardian.
Do you understand?'

And it's no use arguing.
Red, blue or green,
yellow, purple or orange,
that's their balloon
and no one else's.
They are the owner.

So as time goes on
they watch their balloon
with increasing anxiety.
Can it be shrinking?
Is it less shiny?
What's that hissing sound?
Did they do something wrong?

Futile questions!
Some balloons
pop the day they are given,
others last aeons
just getting more wizened.
If you're looking for a reason,
goes one of Balloonland's
wisest sayings,
then apply your own pin.

A Perversion

In the *Proceedings of the Royal Institute of Anthropophagy*
(last year's Spring number, page 132),
there is a most unusual instance recorded
of a man and woman who conspired to eat each other –
and would have done so, had not the laws of nature
    prevented it.
I heartily agree with the writer of the article
who denounces the whole affair as a 'flagrant travesty',
a 'perversion of the established rites' and a 'half-baked stunt'.

Your Biographer

Inevitably
your biographer
is getting it all wrong.

His little screen
recapitulates
the few known facts.

With rapidly dabbing
fingertips he coaxes
a workable pattern, till

there it is —
the truth at last!
And you stand condemned

to centuries
of ignominy,
your well-polished plea unheard.

Synopsis

The novel I propose to write will be
about the size of a late Henry James,
only more airy and accommodating.

The supple interplay of major themes
will furnish it with the exhilarating
sense of a mind meticulous but free.

To catch the voice of truth itself dilating
on the great problems of reality
will be one of my prime technical aims.

A plot that brings the cogency of dreams
to bear on the profoundest tragedy
is already in outline, pending writing.

Love will be treated somewhere, and I see
two figures, naked, in an intimate setting,
although they have not yet been given names.

I hope to start work soon, but am still waiting
for the advance which will ensure my scheme's
otherwise cast-iron viability.

Dreams of Babylon

I hold the book
the one I have been looking for

it tells the truth
in a strange new way

syntax of pentecost
you barely need to read it

rushing to the bloodstream
of its own accord

*

Cubism's collapsing
house of cards

portending a labyrinth
yards and yards

no, miles more like it
of scavengery and botchwork

under a placid light
just so, just so

*

The irreversible machine starts up
and I am in the middle of it

blasting and pounding behind me
scraping in front

exhilarating
to be at its fulcrum

with fluttering fingertips
and tutting tongue

*

Seems we've reached
the inner sanctum

peacocks in a cloister
strut their stuff

they drag their gowns
with a dry luxurious rustle

gaudy poultry
of academe

*

A stocky toddler
and his sumo stomp

green ideograms
of a swiss cheese plant

in apparently fortuitous
juxtaposition

if I had a camera
which I do not

*

To mix a music
out of the night

an electronic psalm
that will assuage all loneliness

from the black hole
a choir of sirens

maximum babel
and the mumbo drums

For Art's Sake

Arbiter

See that man?
You may not know him,
but he carries considerable clout.

Only last week
when he offered his opinion
a reputation tottered.

Art – any art –
is his first love,
and so he prowls the globe
from conference to conference.

There are opera tickets
in his wallet,
a Tiepolo at home.

Be civil to him,
for he is the prince
of a hundred committees
and his fingers loosen bursary-strings.

Klangfarbe

At the first performance
of his twenty-minute sonata
for trombone and lightbulb,

based – so the programme note told us –
on a reading of Jung's
Seelenprobleme der Gegenwart,

the most eloquent detail
and the one I shall remember
beyond all those whomps and rasps and splintered high notes

was the ping of the filament.

Cork Street

In his dream
he had finished a painting,

only one,
but the ultimate statement,

n square feet
of existential brushwork,

and there it hung
in its appointed place:

white wall, polished boards,
with a woman at a desk

and the sense offstage
of pinstripes milling,

captious, legal voices
on the phone from New York

and a fat armoured vehicle
impatient at the gate.

A *Living Sculpture in the Museum without Walls*

For seven years
I tended the shrine,
kept the archives,
swept the floor.

But now she has left me
and the street noise of art history
yammers in my ear.

Howl, Howl

It was a poignant moment:
the old king broken
and that seasoned growl –
the hallmark of so many
memorable commercials –
pitched high and plaintive.

In his arms,
the slack body
of his youngest daughter,
whom I recall
exhibiting her nipples
in some gangland vendetta movie
years back.

The loyal earl
turned his face downstage,
and we knew then
beyond a doubt

that he had justified
the difficult leap
from sitcom
to the legitimate theatre.

Go, Little Book

A grisly marriage
        and a dead-end job;
a misconceived affair
        and its botched curtailment;
no adequate solace
        from parents or children;
hours spent alone
        in the room upstairs
with the neighbours' television
        throbbing through the wall . . .
somehow resulted
        in a little clutch
of wryly-turned
        and unemphatic lyrics,
which a Northern press
        was persuaded to add
to its Autumn list,
        and whose only reviewer –
an Oxford post-graduate
        on the make
in 'literary London' –
        was able to despatch it
in two brisk sentences,
        one containing a joke.

Memres of Alfred Stoker

firs
born X mas day
Yer 1885
in the same burer Waping

pa a way
Ma not
being by Trade merchent Sea man
in forn parts:
all so a precher
on Land

i sow him Latter

4 of 9
not all Livig

a hard Thing Ma sad:
mirs Pale a mid Wife
in the back room bed rom
Nor wod she got Thurgh
when a ANGEL apperd over the JESUS pichire
which i got after
it Savd my Life.

     *

so i name Gabriel
which you did not no why shod you
onlie its Secd
Alfred Gabriel Joseph Stoker
Like that.

some recked she was Ling
but she was not
the ANGEL was Trew.

He had a Gold face she sad
and his Winges Gold flammy
and his ramond of Gold stufes

and in his hand he bare a BIBLE of Gold paper
and his Vois was as the Claper of Thunder over hede
with Gold Litnigg to.

pa rejoyd when he come
and spid the mars Like Candles smut
on the bed room Cornes

Than Ma had Gerge Edie Peg so on
but no ANGEL.

*

Edie was kind
Gerge fot
Peg the devel Mishif
Hennr did:

when 2 i nerle did
i dont remberer

when the Docter come for Hene Harry
Peg stol the Doters hat
but she was Cott:

he being Old whit berd Like the Old King
smild angerlie
give me

Ma sad ile Tan you my girl
pa a way
and she wolop Pege after

Than pa come in he sade wer is harry
and Ma cride
he past over

and pa Lift his Ey on to HEVEN
its a Merce

*

all so 2 older:

Ma sad you woned
for the ANGEL blesing
she rade the BIBLE Storres in bed

Adam Eve Nore
Mose in the baskip
Joseph my name
the buring firy firnes
and the ritig on the Wall
Like at the fish Mogres winnod.

so i ha a game
in Mas cubed

i was Norrer
in the Smells
and the flod out
and i wot to Lagh all Trebling
but i did not

Than Ma buss in and Shew me.

*

pas a venters at Sea as folos
he got in a Tempes at the Cape of Hop
a gret Wale bang his bote at Green Land
and a man eten
pa fell to
Save by a rope
at the noth Pole he saw the Ora Bols sky liths
at Mala he Lay in fever 9 days
and Leches on his hed
in Arab the King gave a cammel Ey to swolaw

and other:

his presens we a big Mask of the Affic devel
Toy animels of Eximo
and a prete Tin box of Egit for Ma

    *

when 7
pa dishage Sack
by the Capten of the Vanese
his Ship at Dar solom
fiting a niger Lasker boy
did not belve in GOD.

so pa call him a wikt Hethen
wher the niger Took a Long nife
and Cut him at the Sholder
with a Skar to see
6 ins glose rinkle
Like a skin of a Lip

and the Capt sade
no coveting on my Ship
when he give pa is papers at the dock

and pa sad Ye:
its a Sine

*

2 Yers preching
waking the Land
Streets rodes
at fares Maket days
in the pub to
GODS WORD

i went

at Epsom darbie race
pa Holed my Hand
for the Gipes
with a Thin dog
the Spake a forn Langige

on a bus Top
Told the pasegers Stand
prase the LORD
but the wod not:
Hop it sun shine

No more

i need a new pensel
difrit culer

*

the river Stech of fith
a man fell in pisend
you her the Ships woo in the fog Monings
the say a Gost of Billie Okins
Lost at Sea

pa prech the Sea men and perrosterturts
when a Spanneck chap rob him for his money
which he do not have
by Gun wof
and cut him with a bottle

Ma mend it.

and Ade gone to Dulge for a Twene
i was Oldis:
Than Gerge Ede Pegge and babe Wilf

and mister Cobit a Loger of the rodes
he had a Tato on his arm
a Mer made
it Swim with a Twick.

*

no Scool to bisie
Lern to read and rite the BIBLE
and drow
all so sing himms
in a good Vois with pa:

Old Cobbit do the Swize box butins
Swoll black wave Like a Sea
Edis wisel pip
in the parler

Throgh a Nith of dowt and Sorew
That
a frend in JESUS
so on

and pa sade on to us
Ye i have a Sine
to covert Scock Land
and the boy Alf to come to
for his ANGEL bidith

and Ma weep
when

To morow

   *

Scock Land

it raned

i dont rember

pa preching on a hill
with a gift of Tonges
a namile cup for monie

the Throw a cabige

*

the house

fers the paler with the moggne Chairs
moslie Shut
ixep Sun day vosens:
you Smell the Old brikes Thur the florry paper

done 3 steps
to the kichin
black rage
Tin pots on hooks
the table rub with viniker

prive at Side:

up Stares
2 beds in frowt

Mas rom pas
a big Cream Yewrer on a Thing
Like a goos

Chimmney

the crikie part you Stan wigling
wer the flor bodes Loos

Cobert in Loft

  *

so Gerge do my nose fitnig
Like you see
all mose Swock flat
jeles of the ANGEL
wich it Yews to be Strait
Like that:

but i drone a pichire of the same ANGEL
on a box
not Gold blake
blak wings black Skie:
wher Gerge rune at
with a devel in his Ey
and hid hit

blod gug evire were

Took to Mas bed
the wormis place
ider done hill
Slep Ther:

   *

i drow the Stores not now to Old
Danile and the King
the pote him in a Lions den gar gar
but the Liked his ear
Jone swolod by a Wale
to do as Told
Jebels the wikid Queen
on a Towr
the thor her done
you get a wosie feel in the bodie
Like on a Swing
and Laseres of the ded
all so Tom Tips boy Sailer
run to Sea
whir the pirets Cote him in a baril
but he wole not Show the Tregers no not he
but Thats difret.

*

That it yews to be
the got it all rong

being a Old ugel gisser with a chines perano
wich you Tern a hand
it jigle a Song

it was not a munnkie
it was a blow parot

    *

Alf me and Groge in own bed
Edie Pege other
Wilf in box
2 dreams.

firs i saw the devel SATAN
him Self:
with a Spike face
Alf he sade
Alf
i Try
onlie a Small pip of er

to week

it hapend a gane

Thes pesil is no good
wobley

   *

its all rite
pece full
ixep the Tee vie
rubige

100 Yers

the done no

*

wher Edie Tech to fly
its esie
Like Thes
She holed my hand and junt:

at Old Sters
so we go crox the river
Like a ANGEL
no flaping

its a mirigle
ha ha:
but the men in the botes
Tell to get done

the Try to Stop us
by a foot
with a Long Stike and a hook
Like at the haber dagers you no

Edie smiles
its nice
Sun day close
hand worm:

*

Than on day pa sad Ye:
i had a Sine
to go on to the Land of Mogro
and prech the pepil Ther
That did evel in the Sith of the LORD
Alf to come to my son
for the hims

but Ma wep saing no
he is but 9
and Little
so pa go on his owen

That we do not see a gen:
onie in a dream some Time
woking for the Land of Moggro
crox the wold
up to Lund Waping
owr Street
at the frot door
up Stares
in the bed room
at the bed

a hoy Alf.

*

moslie for got
to tired
its the pils

Onel some Ties memres
Like you get a wift gravie
for the kichins
in the Monig
10 a clock
it fanick ater.

*

its winter
rember
Jake frost
Snow dirtie
and the river dirtie chugs of ice
ikles on the rops dirte to
and Ma get a coff
Like a kie in a door woned open:

a Lady mises Bussen ded
Stut to a door Step
frosen
and the Skin her face tore of
when the Lift her

Cobet gone
the peles feck him

Ma Took the Swize box to a man of Wite Chaple
2 bob
its a fare price:
and we woke to a fortine Teller
That no the Tea Lees in a yelow cup

i see a Long jirne
what
a serprise

    *

so Ma did
flow to HEVAN
being a Long jirnie
wich the forten Teller Told

a blaket on
and her Hair Lose untidie
Like a BIBLE pirson
and her face Cold.

*

i got the pichire
SWEET JESES

*

the Took us a way
wher i been sence:
in the ofinick firs
Than other

Edie Peg mary
Gerge run to wore
kill by a bom
and Wilf a cabin stewer
on the begum Queen

Send a Letter.

JESUS in dror:
i never see the ANGEL
onlie i no its Trow gospil
which it means I wone die
Like a sun clowid over all glomy
its in the Sky.

Survival: a Patchwork
for Lucinda

If I could borrow
from your intricate art
this one among your accomplishments
a patchwork pattern
words, remnants, savings
things seen and known

        not that old man's
        symbolic map of heaven
        a more questionable symmetry
        looser fabric
        pieced out and negotiated
        day by day by

with the occasional mistake, too
passages jarring
you know why
able to trace
even in lines not quite true
a yearning

        and from your patience
        if I could borrow that
        a more unstinting
        resource than mine
        given to tizzes
        the short hot futile sputter

patience that sits
at the end of the bed
needle plunging
tiny stitches
lips that mime or inaudibly mutter
the primitive arithmetic

       needle and thread
       plunging and tugged taut
       again and again
       plunging the glint
       of purpose and tugged taut
       steady achievement

if I could borrow
as you adjust
the gorgeous sprawl
of work about you
paper templates
jostled rustling

       scraps of poems
       on squares and lozenges
       later to be shed
       for a while lending
       structure and heart
       to your art and mine

       *

To name just some
the African quilts
the Aztec, the Firecracker
the cream and white
and those two sumptuous trophies
gents' old silk ties

in art jargon
colour fields
and you the unflagging labourer
measuring seasons
method and toil
terrain hard-won

as if to occupy
a Klee landscape
who once spoke
of taking a line for a walk
the pertinacious spider
knows the procedure

or you've seen a child
paper flat on floor
inhabiting
the middle of her own drawing
an elbow smudges
lines newly put down

pitched into the making
strange to observe
and an incentive
Klee again
that each should follow
where the pulse of his own heart leads

two pulses
inevitable variance
but music of a kind
the dissonant passages
mutually punitive
yield to sweeter

as when
on the allotment
your design
and most of the work yours
strip pattern
onions, spinach, beetroot, beans

> we keep a distance
> auspicious nonetheless
> to look across
> and catch a glimpse
> through the beanpoles'
> tackle and tangle

> *

A fanning arc
of hose-water plays
over the bean-leaves
drumming rattles
the summer canopy
a gracious dispensation

> you love this narrow
> Utopian plot
> I love it less
> but love you loving it
> nowhere level
> askew on its slope

wrested from the clasp
of couch-grass and bindweed
your discovery
a talent to nurture
blackcurrants and sweet peas
overflowing

who once disparaged
your parents' farm
ironical
growing to recognise
too late
its parched obdurate beauty

too late
the peacocks that shrieked
vindictive queens
from the garage roof
almond-trees writhing
in the combustible orchard

hillside-tilted
under a milder sky
less overwhelming perspective
I watch you tend
with fork and wheelbarrow
our patch

when suddenly
a jangle flung
disembodied
over the rooftops
an ice-cream van
visits the neighbouring estate

stop, start
its musical-chairs
arrangement of Popeye
amplified glockenspiel
conjures children
imagine them hurrying now

*

Best-loved stranger
when the mirror catches us
chancing to pass
embrace and hold
our most ridiculous
photographic grimaces

       looks exchanged
       is that it
       a picture of a marriage
       caught on the hop
       watch the birdie
       then burst out laughing

of course no simple
image will do
the frequently-trumpeted
republic of two
with its improvised constitution
and merry folk-culture

       or sometimes it seems
       obedient
       to peremptory swings
       of climate and temperament
       the jittery ménage
       of a weatherhouse

sickening squalls
electricity shaken
by the passing storm
gulp of vertigo
over the unknown
the unknowable

your illness when
I took refuge
in writing poems
any other subject
you with your
great lonely courage

what then
two solitudes
the grave neighbourly
orbiting of planets
signals dim
as the black hole beckons

no no no
won't do either
stop there
hush typewriter
listen to you busy
in a not distant room

*

Your new beautiful hairstyle
a bushy bob
like Colette's
as soon as I saw it
to meet the ravages
of unsubtle chemotherapy

dashing, girlish
and as it turned out
luckier than some
those poor bald children
at the hospital
their hopeless wigs

resented days
laid-up in bed
Floppy Mop Top
the harsh chemical savour lingering
in your mouth
on breath and kisses

        never again
        you say now
        go through that
        and I say
        amen, amen
        that you never have cause to

yet they looked after you kindly
the sewn gash
by your breast
less elegant
than your artistry
did the trick, though

        and who now minds
        the touch of asymmetry
        Matisse's jaunty drawing
        one breast hitched
        its nipple wider
        for a while

gratitude
for a life mended
yours, ours
rending of fabric
timely bodged
and, of course, anxiety

never again
you say now
though we seldom discuss it
I've seen you finger
the crude seam
painful feeling returns

*

Next holiday
fair stood the wind
down to Provence
our little red Renault
followed its nose
a spiritual homecoming

slipstream blustering
like a flag
at my open window
Normandy, Burgundy
the Auvergne
conceding in their turn

at which time of year
fields of sunflowers
the massed millions
sombre umber faces
yellowing tatters
that gaunt stoop

awaiting inevitable
doom of harvest
and in the vineyards
grapes suspended
heavy as udders
on the maturing vines

pieced and patched
an amplitude of landscape
yielding to enquiry
guidebook and map
those dusty village churches
we love

        where saints and Bible folk
        cluster on the capitals
        in their medieval drag
        agog with life
        death, too, shown
        biding

jaws, fangs and maw
memorably registered
lost souls lined-up
yowl their protest
spirit still recalcitrant
guilty of what

        of merely being
        like you like me
        spinning through a countryside
        stunned by sunlight
        slipstream blustering
        night miles ahead

        *

Those unbidden moments
out of the ordinary
sentimental or visionary
who's to say
stepping into a field once
Mont Ventoux

                    stopping
                    there surrounded
                    by the frisky parabolas
                    of innumerable grasshoppers
                    I thought
                    no, felt

inexplicable elation
a blundering interloper
graciously made welcome
or just ignored
the crazy saint
addresses his insect congregation

                    all part of the pattern
                    spilt landscape
                    hazy sky
                    the car parked out of sight
                    and you in it
                    boulders, thyme

those moments
when the secret seems
about to be given
world on hold
what old Roberto Gerhard called
magic of uneventfulness

                    things just ticking over
                    take them as they come
                    whenever
                    as in Mbabane
                    nightfall
                    the fireflies puffing past

provisional and fleeting
annotations
of a great responsive something
from the orchestra
luminous generous music
or your art

       luminous generous
       the quilt you gave me
       silk ties
       jumble plunder
       how many months in the making
       that epiphany

       *

Well, you've survived
touch wood
so far
illness, marriage
the lesser tribulations
we've survived

       and this poem here
       not much more
       than to say I'm glad
       an emulous tribute
       matching and patching
       the pattern borrowed

8 x 8
a dabbling in primal symmetries
hope even of catching
in the midst of it all
the drift
the changes

two bookworms in bed
slow piecemeal understanding
you once more engrossed
in your eternal Proust
the mark advances
a page or two

then sleep
or the arbitrary patterns of love
interface
of kiss and kiss
urgent fluent reciprocations
rapture answering

and what of those hours apart
overlapped perhaps
by the insubstantial
quick-unpicked-at
self-deconstructing
patchwork of dreams

your art
stuff of the day-to-day
single-minded creation
that moment near completion
when you spread it all out
on the sitting-room floor

hardly room
this tiny flat
for the flaunting of sudden colour
almost to the skirting-board
you squatting in the middle
smoothing it smoothing it true

Cold Snap
for my father

A crossword left undone,
a dictionary undisturbed –
the evening he arrived
through landscapes mute with snow
to attend his mother's woe –
reminded the tongue-tied son
of a long-standing debt
now never to be paid.

Only here let it be said
how much his primitive awe
of words, his cryptic style,
his thinking it worthwhile
to lay his poor musings out
in patterns, down and across,
owe to your verbal wit –
though it won't offset any loss
or bring on the great thaw.